being a fashion stylist

Isabel Thomas

Lerner Publications Company
Minneapolis

First American edition published
in 2013 by Lerner Publishing
Group, Inc. Published by
arrangement with Wayland, a
division of Hachette Children's
Books

Lerner Publications Company
A division of Lerner Publishing Group, Inc.
241 First Avenue North
Minneapolis, MN U.S.A.

Website address: www.lernerbooks.com

Library of Congress
Cataloging-in-Publication Data

Thomas, Isabel, 1980–
    Being a fashion stylist / by Isabel Thomas.
       p.   cm. — (On the radar: awesome jobs)
    Includes index.
      ISBN: 978-0-7613-7778-8 (lib. bdg. : alk. paper)
       1. Fashion—Vocational guidance—Juvenile
    literature. 2. Clothing trade—Vocational guidance—
    Juvenile literature. 3. Fashion designers—Vocational
    guidance—Juvenile literature. I. Title.
    TT507.T467 2013
    746.9′2023—dc23   2011052675

Manufactured in the United States of America
 – CG – 7/15/12

Acknowledgments: Dreamstime: Featureflash 23br; Getty Images:
Digital Vision 1, Jon Kopaloff 10, Evans Vestal Ward/NBC Universal/
Bravo 11tl, 18–19, JB Lacroix 20bl, Robyn Beck 23bc; WireImage 14,
27; Istockphoto: Andipantz 13, Izabela Habur 12–13; Lenya Jones:
22b, 24c, 24r, 24–25, 25l, 25c; Melis Kuris: 23, 23bl; Shutterstock: Arvzdix
2r, 11b, Sandra Cunningham 28–29, DSPA 30bl, Helga Esteb 17t, 17b,
20–21, Fashion B 30l, Raisa Kanareva 9, Nina Malyna 11tr, Luba V Nel
31r, Losevsky Pavel 8, Lev Radin 21r, Joe Seer 3br, 7, Kiselev Andrey
Valerevich cover, 30br, Vipflash 2t, 4–5, Debby Wong 11bl, 16–17;
Wikipedia: 6, Manuel Bartual 31b..

Main body text set in
Helvetica Neue LT Std 13/15.5.
Typeface provided by Adobe Systems.

cover stories

thepeople

theart

thetalk

Best dressed

A fashion stylist may take years to build a good reputation. Many start by styling celebrities and models for magazines, films, or television shows. They learn dressmaking skills and become experts in putting together the right clothes to create a fabulous effect for celebs such as Lady Gaga *(above)*. Top stylists can create looks that suit both the person and the event perfectly. They get their clients on the best-dressed lists time after time.

STAR STYLE

Celebrities are rarely photographed in the same clothes twice. How do they put together so many fresh, trendy outfits? Most have a secret weapon: a stylist. It is their job to come up with the perfect look for every appearance.

Image is everything

Celebrity stylists do not just choose clothes. They help their clients create an image that wins them media attention, fans, and work. Stylists know their clients inside out. They understand how clothes work on different body shapes, and they choose clothes that fit well and look great.

Get the look

Most celebrity public appearances, from red-carpet events to working out at the gym, are carefully styled. Readers of magazines, newspapers, and blogs expect to see different outfits every time, so stylists are constantly working to create new looks. The best stylists do not just follow fashion trends: they make them. Stylists influence boutique fashion too. When fashion fans see an A-list star looking great, they want to copy the look. Stores may base a whole collection around one famous person's style.

Fashion and fame

Stylists have the power to turn products into must-have items. When fashion designers invite stars and their stylists to design shows, they hope that the celebrity will buy the clothes and then be photographed wearing them. In turn, this could create a following of fashion fans. The best stylists may help designers with new collections and can even start their own fashion lines.

STYLE STORY

From kings and queens to the first movie stars, the rich and famous have always employed experts to help them dress well. During the twentieth century, stylists helped sell clothes to the masses by making the pieces look good at fashion shows and in magazines. Modern stylists are some of the most influential people in fashion.

Charles Frederick Worth (1826–1895) was the first designer to advise and dress his aristocratic clients, including Elisabeth von Österreich, empress of Austria *(above)*.

Rich and famous

The first style consultants were personal assistants who helped wealthy people dress well. The best-dressed aristocrats set style trends that were copied by other wealthy people. Rich women wore custom-made outfits with many layers. They needed help to get dressed, from putting on enormous petticoats to fastening corsets. In the 1800s and the early 1900s, photographs of society events appeared in early fashion magazines, showing the latest clothes worn by royalty and aristocrats. Before the age of professional models, readers looked at these celebrities to find out what was fashionable.

Shop the style

The invention of the sewing machine in the mid-1800s led to clothes that were sold ready-to-wear. Department stores began to offer the services of personal shoppers, helping customers find clothes that suited them. Stores also used style consultants to help them order the most fashionable stock. In the 1910s, newspaper reporters invented the word *stylist* to describe the job of Tobé Davis, a style expert who advised hundreds of department stores on what would be in fashion each season.

Fashion and film

From the 1930s, the most famous faces and figures in the world belonged to Hollywood movie stars, and it soon became important for these celebrities to look good all the time. Since then, stylists have been in demand in Los Angeles, but the celebrity stylist phenomenon really exploded in the 1990s. Designers wanted the most famous actors to wear their clothes. The actors knew that a fashionable image would help them get work. Stylists became the bridge between celebrity and designer, setting up deals between stars and fashion brands.

Power players

Top celebrity stylists such as Rachel Zoe have become household names. Their celebrity partnerships give them huge power and influence in the fashion industry. In 2011 Lady Gaga's stylist Nicola Formichetti became the first stylist to be put in charge of design at a large fashion brand, when he was named the creative director of Thierry Mugler (a French fashion label).

Rachel Zoe *(pictured)* is one of the most influential people in Hollywood fashion and employs a team of seven people to help get her celebrity looks just right.

The Rachel Zoe effect

Rachel Zoe tops the list of the world's most influential stylists. As well as dressing A-list clients such as Cameron Diaz, Zoe consults for fashion brands. She has written a best-selling book and stars in a reality TV show, *The Rachel Zoe Project.* She has even started her own fashion label, bringing her famous "hippy-meets-vintage" style to the mass-market.

WORD ON STYLE

Add some style to your fashion speak with the On the Radar guide!

best-dressed lists

the lists compiled by magazines, newspapers, and websites, picturing the most stylish celebrities at an event or out and about. Being on these lists gives the celebrities good publicity.

boutique

a small or speciality fashion store selling selected clothes and accessories

costume design

researching, designing, and creating costumes for a character in TV shows, on film, or onstage

creative director

someone who oversees every part of a performer's image, from clothes to the theme of his or her music and shows

custom made

something that has been made specifically for a celebrity

fashion director

the top stylist working on a magazine. The fashion director controls which clothes, models, and brands make it into the magazine and decides how they are presented to make them appealing to readers.

fashion editor

a stylist working on a magazine or newspaper

fashion forward

people, clothes, or looks that are very fashionable and ahead of the trends

fashionista

someone who follows fashion very closely

fashion PR

short for fashion public relations. The fashion PR person is responsible for making sure that the fashion house is always presented in the best possible way and is usually the link between the fashion house and stylists.

personal stylist

a stylist who is paid to style people for public or private events, or everyday life, rather than for a photo shoot, a film, or a TV show

Designer clothes are often sold in exclusive shops or boutiques.

props

portable things such as furniture or accessories that are used at a photo shoot

signature look

a trademark way of dressing for which a celebrity is known

tear sheets

examples of previously published work in a stylist's portfolio

test shoot

a photo shoot that a stylist works on for free to gain experience. The test shoot is not for publication, but it helps the stylist build a portfolio that will bring him or her work in the future.

vintage

original clothes or accessories from the past

GLOSSARY

A-list

a real or imaginary list of the most "important" individuals, especially in show business

aristocrats

members of the highest class in some societies

choreography

a planned sequence of dance moves

client

someone who pays a stylist to work for him or her

collaborating

working together to produce or create something

complexion

the natural color, texture, and appearance of a person's skin

corsets

close-fitting undergarments that support and shape the waistline, hips, and breasts

icon

a person who is a symbol of devotion or admiration

internship

a job (often unpaid) that helps someone gain experience in an industry

mainstream fashion

clothing and accessories that are not exclusive to designer shops but can be bought in most cities

Fashion editors can push the boundaries to make clothes as eye-catching as possible.

paparazzi

the photographers who follow celebrities to get unofficial, unposed photographs of them

petticoats

thin slips or underskirts worn beneath skirts and dresses

source

to look for something

MAKING IT

From choosing red-carpet dresses to planning a film's costumes, a stylist works with celebrities in several different ways.

Dressing the stars

Celebrities use stylists to help them plan everyday wardrobes as well as red-carpet looks. Personal stylists also help rising stars develop a signature look. Stylists learn what suits their clients and help them maintain trendsetting looks, making sure the paparazzi never get a bad picture.

With the help of her stylist, Emma Stone often tops the best-dressed lists.

Making up stories

Stylists such as Katie Grand, who work for magazines or newspapers, are known as fashion editors or fashion directors. Part of their job is styling models and celebrities for photo shoots. These stylists help create a story that shows both the star and the products at their best. Each shoot can take weeks of planning, and a top stylist can expect to earn $50,000 for a celebrity fashion shoot.

Looking the part

Costume designers are stylists who create film character looks. Getting a character's look right can involve a lot of research—costume designers create anything from vampires to gangsters. The clothes worn in popular shows set fashion trends, and some actors have become famous for their screen style. For example, *Gossip Girl* stylist Eric Daman has turned cast members Blake Lively and Leighton Meester into fashion icons.

Image makers

The stage outfits worn by pop icons such as Lady Gaga, Beyoncé, and Rihanna shape their strong images. To get it right, celebrities hire creative or artistic directors to style every part of a show, from costumes to choreography. Top creative directors, such as William Baker, can be just as important to a musician's career as a record producer and publicity agent.

Fashion editors direct photo shoots to help create a theme that complements the clothes.

Beyoncé *(above)* and Rihanna *(left)* use artistic directors to create an onstage style that suits their songs.

IMAGE MAKERS

A celebrity stylist works as a vital member of a large team to put together a fashion shoot. Once the look and approach of a shoot have been decided, the stylist sources clothes, shoes, and accessories.

The superstar

Celebrities know that fresh, eye-catching photographs will help interest fans in their latest work. The stylist provides a rack of clothes so that the celebrity can choose outfits that keep with the mood of the photo shoot.

When working on a celebrity shoot for a magazine, a stylist works closely with a team of editors, designers, and stylists from the magazine to plan the perfect look.

The stylist

It's not just the celebrity who has to look good. A key part of a stylist's job is to make clothes and accessories look so desirable in the finished picture that people will want to buy them. Stylists steam clothes to remove any creases, polish jewelry, and then help the celebrity to dress, pinning or sewing garments around the body for the very best fit.

The photographer

On the day of the shoot, the stylist works with the photographer to bring his or her vision to life. This includes styling the background and props, such as furniture or plants, to create the right mood and character.

The hair and makeup stylists

Hair and makeup complete the look that the stylist creates. Hair and makeup stylists take inspiration from the clothes and must balance the latest trends with a style that suits the celebrity's complexion and face shape.

The fashion PR

Fashion PRs promote fashion brands. They lend clothes and accessories to stylists for free, in return for coverage in magazines. This is why celebrities are often photographed wearing the latest gear not yet in stores.

BRITT BARDO

Superstar stylist

Britt won the Star Stylist award at the 2009 Hollywood Life's Style Awards. Britt says her goal is to make her clients look "super-relaxed and effortless."

From farming to fashion

Britt Bardo grew up in a small farming town where there were few fashion stores. But she found creative ways to be fashionable, such as using colored paper clips as earrings! When she was 18, she moved to Detroit, Michigan, and trained to be a photographer at the city's College for Creative Studies. After finishing her degree, she moved to New York City in search of work.

Big break

In New York, Britt soon realized that styling photo shoots would be the best way to combine her love of fashion and her knowledge of what makes a great picture. She first worked as a sales assistant in the designer jeans shop G-Star in New York. Then she spent three years assisting celebrity stylist Andrea Lieberman, whose clients included Gwen Stefani and Jennifer Lopez. Britt's big break came when J. Lo asked her to be her personal stylist.

Career highlights

2004 styled the Jennifer Lopez music video for "Get Right"

2006 *Forbes* magazine called her a "superstar stylist"

2007 styled the Mariah Carey music video for "Lil L.O.V.E"

2008 styled the Hilary Duff music video for "Reach Out"

2010 signed as fashion consultant for eBay

Fashion fun

Britt quickly became known for her fun attitude toward fashion, and she won more famous clients, including actress Kate Hudson and stars Mary-Kate and Ashley Olsen. Britt helped the Olsen twins work out their "scruffy chic" look, transforming them into fashion icons.

In demand

Britt has become a stylist to A-list stars such as Cameron Diaz and Blake Lively. While her job has glamorous perks, such as hanging out with celebrity clients, in her spare time, Britt likes to scuba dive and spend time with her family. Her career may have skyrocketed, but her feet are very firmly on the ground!

THE STATS

Name: Britt Bardo
Place of birth: Lima, Ohio
Lives: Los Angeles and New York City
Job: Hollywood stylist and fashion consultant

RED-CARPET TRICKS

On the Radar reveals the stylists' tricks that keep celebrities looking perfectly groomed on the red carpet.

1. Wig tape

The double-sided sticky tape used to keep wigs in place is a last-minute style saver. Wig tape has amazing holding power and can be cut to any shape. Stylists use it to mend broken hemlines, stick feathers or flowers in place, and keep clothes in the right place as the celebrity waves to the crowd.

2. Needle and nylon thread

If Blake Lively (*pictured*) looks as if she is sewn into her dress, she probably is! Stylists always have a needle and strong thread on hand to mend broken zippers, straps, or jewelry. Clear nylon thread is invisible to the cameras, so no one will know that the star had to be cut out of her outfit at the end of the night!

3. Sandpaper

New shoes are great for the red carpet, but slippery soles and soft carpet can add up to disaster. Stylists use sandpaper to scratch the bottom of shoes and prevent slipping.

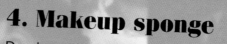

4. Makeup sponge

Deodorant is a must for nerve-racking award shows, which involve sitting for hours under hot lights. Celebrity stylists have a clever trick to remove deodorant marks from expensive dresses. A clean and dry makeup sponge can remove white marks gently without needing to use water. The sponges are small enough for the star to slip into her handbag for emergency touch-ups.

5. Dryer sheet

On a hot, dry day, flyaway hair can ruin a celebrity's red-carpet look. Some stylists use a bizarre trick. They touch the hair very lightly with a dryer sheet. This gets rid of the static electricity that creates frizz, just like it does with the laundry. Vanessa Hudgens's locks (*left*) look red-carpet ready!

WILLIAM BAKER

THE STATS

Name: William Baker
Born: 1973
Place of birth: Manchester, England
Nationality: British
Job: Personal stylist and creative director

Stylish start

William grew up in Manchester, England. In the 1980s, the stylish city was home to world-famous nightclubs and bands. William became well known on the style scene. But he also worked hard at school. He loved fashion, so he worked part-time as a sales assistant for the legendary British designer Vivienne Westwood.

Creative genius

William's creative ideas changed Kylie's image and helped to relaunch her career. He was promoted from stylist to creative director. As well as styling Kylie's music videos and public appearances, he has directed award-winning shows such as KylieFever2002. Kylie's concerts have become famous for their breathtaking stage costumes, choreography, and sets. In 2008 William won a style award from the fashion magazine *Elle*.

Meeting Kylie

In 1994 pop star Kylie Minogue (*above, with William*) came into the Vivienne Westwood boutique, and William asked her out for coffee. Although William did not have any formal fashion training, he wowed Kylie with his style ideas. Over the next year, they became friends. His first official styling job came in 1995, when Kylie was set to perform with Nick Cave and the Bad Seeds on a British prime-time TV show called *Top of the Pops*. William teamed Kylie's messy red hair with a green silk dress covered in beetles. Kylie invited William to style her for more performances and music videos, and her new looks made headlines over and over again.

In demand

Many stars want to work with William. He has styled tours for other musicians, including Britney Spears's Circus tour in 2009 and Leona Lewis's Labyrinth tour in 2010. William describes his job as "a bit of everything. Photography, styling, directing shows and videos, writing . . . If I had to do just one of those things, I'd get frustrated."

STYLE PRO TIPS

The best stylists use accessories such as bags, belts, and jewelry to maximum effect. They work with clients such as Emma Watson (pictured) to create looks that show off their best features. Celebrity stylists spend hours working with their clients to find a style that works for them. Try out these top tips to transform your own wardrobe.

1. Customize!

Great stylists carry a sewing kit so that they can customize an outfit by adding their own special touches. They may change buttons to immediately update a piece of clothing or dramatically transform it by altering the neck- or hemline.

2. Vintage vibe

Celebrity stylists are often seen in vintage clothing shops, searching for hidden classic gems. They mix older items with the very latest accessories to create a fabulous vintage look that reflects the latest fashion trends.

3. Mix and match

Many stylists love mixing various shades and textures of the same color. For instance, they may pair a navy suit with a slate-blue shirt and a blue tweed tie. The chosen shades and textures are subtly different so that they work together. But the pieces do not look as though the celebrity is wearing matching clothes from head to toe.

Chloë Moretz mixes textures with fun stripes for a perfect match!

4. Shave and save

Fluff and loose thread can make a vintage piece of clothing look shabby. Stylists use a razor to shave the surface of old fabric. This gets rid of any loose threads or fluffy wool and breathes new life into an older garment.

5. Showing off!

Stylists focus on their clients' most attractive features. They'll emphasize a small waist by accentuating it with an eye-catching, colorful belt. If a celebrity has great legs, they'll show them off in a dazzling short skirt. While top stylists follow trends, they don't follow them to the letter. They shape their celebrities' outfits to work with trends in a way that flatters the client.

MELIS KURIS

On the Radar expert Melis Kuris has styled Anna Paquin, Jordin Sparks, Ashley Greene, Lily Collins, and Taylor Lautner.

What got you interested in fashion?

Growing up in Turkey, I would change my outfit at least five times a day for every occasion. I collected vintage fashion, including great pieces that my parents bought in the 1960s and 1970s, from Hermès scarves to Gaultier suits.

How did you become a celebrity stylist?

When I was 18, I moved to Los Angeles, California, and started working for different stylists. It was so much fun styling models for shoots and shows! I realized then that styling could be a career path for me.

What are the best parts of your job?

Every day is different, so I never get tired of working. I'm constantly collaborating with new people. One highlight of my career so far was working with most of the cast of *Twilight*. That job completely changed my career, and I am so grateful for the experience.

Does your job have any downsides?

The downside of being a stylist is that everyone has an opinion on your work. So, you have to have tough skin and stay true to yourself. You have to have confidence in what you are talking about.

What helps someone succeed in fashion styling?

Being organized. We constantly have to check in and check out clothes with fashion houses and handle receipts. If you lose something, you have to pay for it.

What advice do you have for someone wanting to become a stylist?

Never turn down a job. Ever. It doesn't matter if it pays a lot or absolutely nothing. If you take on a job, it may lead to something bigger.

What's next in your career?

I like to dabble in a little bit of everything, including personal styling, magazines, advertising campaigns, commercials, music videos, TV, and fashion shows. I just finished costume designing my first film, which was exciting. I like to be the stylist who always says, 'Yes, I've done that!'

Lily Collins, Jordin Sparks, and Taylor Lautner (*pictured left to right*) are just a few of Melis's famous clients.

HOLLYWOOD DREAMS

My story by Lenya Jones

I've always loved fashion, but at first, I didn't know how I could make a career out of it. When I was younger, I worked as a marketing assistant at a famous department store that was often featured in fashion magazines. I started to get ideas about styling, and one of my managers persuaded me to try my hand at it.

To get a better understanding of the job, I started assisting stylists. Assisting is the best way to learn because you get hands-on experience. When I felt I was ready, I started approaching photographers and began test shooting like crazy. Then, a magazine called *Cherrie* asked me to organize its fashion section. After that, I was hired to style more fashion spreads, and my work appeared in magazines regularly.

Next, a TV director asked me to work on the wardrobe for a TV pilot. I was lucky enough to work with a world-famous assistant director and a great producer, who recommended me for other projects, including a short film. After that, I worked on several films and TV ads, dressing the stars and making everyone look great. My first feature film *Dealing with Destiny* (2011) even premiered at the Cannes Film Festival.

These days I'm pursuing more costume designing opportunities in Hollywood, and I plan to move to Los Angeles. With perseverance and determination, I hope to hold the Oscar for Best Costume Design in the near future! My best advice is: don't give up. If you really love styling, just go for it!

Lenya styled this model's transformation from redheaded guy-next-door to blue-haired being.

KATIE GRAND

Fashion's ultimate fan

THE STATS

Name: Katie Grand
Place of birth: Leeds, England
Lives: London, England
Job: Stylist, magazine editor, and fashion consultant

Self-styled talent

Katie's passion for fashion started when she was 12. Her father bought her copies of the style magazines *Vogue* and the *Face*. Overnight, she changed from "nerdy" child into a wannabe fashion designer. Katie was not good at art, but she took drawing and pottery classes to improve her design skills.

Getting into magazines

When Katie was 17, she wrote to the editor of *Vogue* to ask how to get a job. Katie followed the editor's advice and went to study art at college. Before finishing school, Katie left to work on the magazine *Dazed & Confused*. She worked there for seven years and so impressed the editors of rival magazine the *Face* that they gave her the job of fashion director.

High fashion

Katie hit the big time in 1998 when luxury handbag company Bottega Veneta hired her to give them a new image. Katie used young designer Giles Deacon to turn Bottega Veneta's fashion shows into must-see events. Her work captured the attention of Prada, who hired Katie as their chief stylist. Katie went on to style ads and fashion shows for dozens of top designers. She has also put together cover-star looks for A-list celebrities such as Madonna, Kate Moss, Scarlett Johansson, Christina Ricci, and Victoria Beckham.

Super stylist

Katie has become one of the most powerful stylists in the world, earning $4,600 to $6,200 a day. She also runs her own style magazine, *LOVE*, for people who love fashion and design. Katie was offered a job designing handbags for Mulberry, but she decided to stick with what she does best—being a stylist.

Career highlights

1984 read her first copy of the *Face*

1992 went to work on *Dazed & Confused* magazine

1999 became fashion director of the *Face*

2000 made editor in chief of fashion and art magazine *Pop*

2005 named as one of the world's most powerful stylists by the *Daily Telegraph* (London)

2009 launched *LOVE* fashion magazine

Katie works in partnership with celebrities and designers and is one of the most powerful people in the fashion industry.

MILLION-DOLLAR LOOKS

$6,000

The highest daily fee charged by a celebrity stylist in the weeks before the Oscars.

21

The number of dresses that website InStyle chose to feature from Taylor Swift's best looks in honor of her twenty-first birthday. The musician loves dresses, and stylists often select successful ones for her.

3

The number of hours it takes to style a female star's makeup and hair for a red-carpet ceremony.

$11,000

The cost of hair styling, makeup, eyelash extensions, and spray tanning for celebrities on Oscar day.

80

The percent of Hollywood stylist Nicole Chavez's clients who get to keep their gowns after a red-carpet event.

$30,000

The amount earned by a top costume designer per project.

$50,000

The amount earned by an elite stylist for several weeks' work planning a fashion shoot with a celebrity client.

ALL GLAMOUR AND GLITZ?

Celebrity styling sounds like every fashion lover's dream job. From the outside, it looks just as glamorous as being a celebrity. The benefits include these:

YES

1. Turning a love of clothes and fashion into a career! Stylists have to develop a vast knowledge of trends past and present. This means doing things for work that other people do for fun, such as watching films, going to gigs, and shopping for clothes and accessories.
2. Traveling to exotic locations. From finding the perfect location for a photo shoot to jetting to fashion shows around the world, international travel is a must.
3. Being creative. Anyone can buy clothes, but celebrity stylists combine them in original and fashion-forward ways. Top stylists such as Katie Grand are so creative that their ideas influence designers.
4. Seeing your ideas and work in print. Successful stylists have the satisfaction of seeing the images they help to create in magazines, newspapers, and fashion blogs.
5. Working with like-minded people. Stylists need contacts inside the fashion industry, including models, makeup artists, hairstylists, photographers, and fashion PRs. Networking at fashion parties and events is a glamorous but important part of the role.

NO

However, stylists are quick to point out how hard they work. It can be a long time before the job becomes glamorous. The downsides include these:

1. Many stylists start out as unpaid interns at magazines. They work with photographers on a large number of test shoots to get tear sheets and build a portfolio. It can be two years or more before a stylist starts making money.

2. Working in the world of photo shoots, films, or TV shows can mean long days, tight deadlines, and often time away from home on shoots. It is the stylist's job to fit in with the client's schedule. Stylists may be on call for a demanding celebrity, or they may work 18 hours a day to prepare for a big event. All this leaves stylists little time for a social life of their own!

3. Celebrity stylists are responsible for everything that goes into a flawless look, including steaming clothes and keeping up with paperwork. Packing and lugging suitcases around is hard work. Stylists also need to learn how to sew, so they can make every item fit and look good on the body.

4. Not all style is about glamour. Indie bands such as Athlete and Starsailor hire stylists to create an "unstyled" image! You won't find these stylists interviewed in the press or posing next to their clients on the red carpet.

YES OR NO?

Stylists work in a glamorous industry, but getting there takes effort, teamwork, and years of experience. They are the ones mending clothes and doing the laundry, while their celebrity clients step out in the spotlight. But elite stylists love their jobs because they give them a chance to live and breathe style—and even shape fashion history themselves!

GET MORE INFO

Books

Colson, Mary. *Being a Makeup Artist*. Minneapolis: Lerner Publications Company, 2012. Learn about the exciting careers of makeup artists.

Dressing a Nation: The History of U.S. Fashion series. Minneapolis: Twenty-First Century Books, 2012. Beautiful and sometimes bizarre U.S. fashions are covered in this series.

Maxwell, Kim. *Career Diary of a Fashion Stylist*. Herndon, VA: Garth Gardner Company, 2007. Kim shares the ins and outs of being a fashion stylist.

McAssley, Jacqueline, and Claire Buckley. *Basics Fashion Design: Styling*. Lausanne, Switzerland: AVA Publishing, 2011. This book looks at all the different aspects of fashion in which stylists can be involved.

Morrison, Sasha Charnin. *Secrets of Stylists: An Insider's Guide to Styling the Stars*. San Francisco: Chronicle Books, 2011. Read this book for celebrity stylists' interviews and advice.

Thomas, Isabel. *Being a Photographer*. Minneapolis: Lerner Publications Company, 2012. Explore the awesome job of photographer in this book.

Websites

Costume Designers Guild
http://www.costumedesignersguild .com/news/
Read up on what costume designers have to say, check out some of their costumes and designs, and access past issues of the *Costume Designer* magazine.

The Cut
http://nymag.com/daily/fashion/
Check out the *New York Times Magazine*'s fashion blog to keep up to date on all the new trends!

Street Peeper
http://streetpeeper.com/
Visit this fashion blog to see what's hot and happening around the world.

INDEX